The Biggest Tax Cheat In America Is the I.R.S.

*One Taxpayer's Audit
of Our Income Tax System—
And How It Has Destroyed
Free Enterprise
And Personal Freedom
in This Country*

With Penalties Assessed to the I.R.S. for—
Taxpayer Abuse
Arrogance
Unconstitutional Actions
Brutality

OTHER BOOKS BY CARL JAPIKSE:

The Tao of Meow
Fart Proudly
Pigging Out in Columbus
Teeing Off in Central Ohio
Exploring the Tarot
The Light Within Us

The Biggest Tax Cheat In America Is the I.R.S.

*An Inquiry
by Carl Japikse*

ENTHEA PRESS
Atlanta, Georgia — Columbus, Ohio

There is only one difference between the tax collector and the taxidermist—the taxidermist leaves the hide.
—M. Caplin, former director of the IRS

ISBN 0-89804-811-7

Contents

TO THE MEMORY
OF ALEX COUNCIL,
A TRUE AMERICAN MARTYR

Shelling Out
for Uncle Sam

Imagine, if you will, the United States of America without an income tax. April 15 would be just another day in the year. There would be no Internal Revenue Service. No withholding. No complicated forms to fill out. No penalties if you forgot to report something—or didn't understand the instructions. More money in your paycheck every payday—perhaps enough to put into a savings account, like people used to do. And the best part of all—that savings account wouldn't be taxed, as it is today.

Sound like a fantasy—the hallucinations of a modern day Don Quixote tilting at windmills? Aren't taxes inevitable—death and taxes, and all that?

Yes, taxes are inevitable—but income taxes are not. As recently as 80 years ago, there was no income tax in the United States. In fact, Congress was *prohibited* from levying an income tax by the Constitution as it was originally written and approved by our Founding Fathers. There were property taxes, excise taxes, and sales taxes; the revenue the government needed to operate had to be raised one way or another. But there was no income tax.

Somehow, for most of the first 140 years of our history as a country, the federal government managed to operate without an income tax. In fact, many people would argue that it actually served the public better in those pre-tax years than ever since. But that is a matter of opinion. The fact remains that America became the great nation it is—a world power—without an income tax. It bought the Louisiana Purchase without an income tax; it financed the construction of the Panama Canal without an income tax. It settled the West without an income tax.

But politicians are seldom happy with what they have; they tend to want what they have not. So, in the late 19th century, our representatives decided that we needed an income tax. They wanted more money to spend.

They established one in 1894, but the Supreme Court quickly ruled it unconstitutional. The issue was put on the back burner awhile, until 1909, when Congress passed a constitutional amendment making it legal to impose such a tax. The amendment was sent to the states to be ratified. By 1913, enough states had ratified the measure to make it a part of the Constitution. Our protection was gone. We, the same people who had rebelled against taxation without representation, had willingly sacrificed a highly important economic freedom. Congress immediately enacted the new tax, and we have been stuck with the income tax ever since.

Sane people might wonder how the American public allowed itself to be hoodwinked into approving this amendment? How could so many otherwise intelligent people actually vote in favor of such a burden?

The answer makes most sense if compared to a shell game. In a common shell game, a con artist has three walnut shells and a pea. He moves the shells about, challenging suckers to bet on which shell contains the pea. Of course, none of the shells does—he palms the pea so that it never appears. In this way, he wins every bet.

On the issue of the income tax, the principal con artist was Cordell Hull, a congressman from Tennessee who later became secretary of state under Franklin Roosevelt. By the early 1900's, manufacturing interests in the East had persuaded Congress to enact heavy tariffs on imported goods, thereby protecting their own sales. Folks in the South and West disliked the tariffs, as they gained no benefit from them. Hull felt the same way, and managed to get an income tax tacked onto yet another tariff bill.

In secret, President Howard Taft and Hull worked out a deal: if Hull dropped the income tax from the tariff bill, Taft and the Republican Party would support a constitutional amendment creating an income tax. Taft figured the country would never be so nearsighted as to ratify the amendment, once it passed Congress. But he was wrong. Hull had palmed the pea— and we are stuck with the results.

Actually, the tax plan that was implemented in 1913 was remarkably tame. The initial tax rate was just one percent—that's right, just one percent—and it was only imposed on incomes of more than $3,000 for single people, $4,000 for married people. In 1913, an annual income of $3,000 was an extremely good salary, comparing to one of $35,000 today. The $4,000 allowed for a married couple compares to $47,000 today. As a result, less than five percent of the population actually ended up paying any taxes under this program. Most Americans—including the entire middle class—paid no income taxes at all.

Who can blame the American public for passing an amendment that would produce such a tame tiger of a tax? It's easy to see what has happened since—but it's hard to blame the public for voting its pocketbook.

Taxes went up sharply during World War I, but fell to moderate levels during the Roaring Twenties. Even as late as 1939, only five percent of all Americans were obligated to pay income tax. And there was no withholding. So far, we seemed to be winning the shell game.

But then World War II came—and the need for much more revenue to support the war effort. The government quickly expanded the income tax base to include the whole middle class and even the lower classes. Six million taxpayers in

1939 became fifty million in 1945. And the rates ranged from 23 percent on the low end to a whopping 94 percent on the high end.

Few people complained even then, because they recognized the needs of the war effort. But they expected the rates to drop sharply after the war was over.

This is when our government took us for a sucker. We expected the pea to be under at least one of the shells, but it wasn't under any of them! The government palmed the pea. Instead of lowering the taxes back to prewar levels, the government kept them almost as high as during the war. During the 1950's, the tax rate reached a range of 22 percent on the low end and 92 percent on the high end. Some of the rates have dropped in the decades since, but Congressional manipulation of deductions and limitations has kept the tax bite virtually the same.

Many reasons have been given: the cold war, the cost of military preparedness, entitlement programs, and so on. But two facts remain:

1. Once a politician has dipped his hand into the public's pocket, it's almost impossible for him to take it back out; and—

2. We the people have been suckered by one of the biggest con games in history.

Lulled into believing that an income tax would only affect a small percentage of our income—and not even that unless we made a lot of money—we consented to a basic change in the Constitution which has now been used to justify a monstrosity:

• Unacceptably high tax rates.

• A tax system that is being used routinely in ways that have nothing to do with raising revenues for the government.

• A tax system which puts the burden of collecting taxes on ourselves—at the risk of crushing penalties and criminal action.

• A tax system that annually bilks us out of billions of dollars that are rightfully ours.

• A tax system that presumes that we the taxpayers are guilty, *even after we have proven ourselves innocent!*

• A tax system that turns ordinary taxpayers into criminals and wrecks the lives of thousands of average Americans every year.

• A tax system that costs us billions of dollars each year in order to comply with its demands.

But as devastating as playing the shell game has become, it is not something we have to continue to accept. The suckers who are conned by a street shell game are willing victims. We may not have realized how much the income tax system is a con—but once we know it, we do not have to continue to accept it.

Having once given up a basic freedom, we can demand it back. At the very least, we can demand that our government stop abusing this freedom in ways we never anticipated.

The first step lies in understanding that we have been conned—and are still being conned. We were conned by Congress into letting it change the Constitution, and we are still being conned, each year as we fill out our tax returns.

We are conned into paying taxes we do not owe. Not just a dollar here or there, but billions of dollars every year.

The shell game is still in progress. It is run by the Internal Revenue Service. We the taxpayers are the suckers, shelling out for Uncle Sam.

And we will continue to be—until we stand up and demand some simple, sensible changes.

We, the Tax Collectors

In ancient societies, the king or pharaoh hired tax collectors who would travel from town to town to gather the levies due the crown. These taxes were often based on the amount of land a person owned, but sometimes they were calculated as a percentage of harvest produced.

These tax collectors often took the law into their own hands in order to collect these monies, and frequently treated the citizenry quite brutally. As a result, the tax collector—or "tax farmer" as he was sometimes known—was usually universally hated.

One of the problems of our modern system is that it eliminates this highly visible middle man, the tax collector. We are expected to be our own tax collector! Each April, or more frequently if we are self-employed, we are expected to tell the IRS far more about ourselves and our financial

15

condition than any government or governmental agency has a right—or a genuine need—to know. We are expected to become experts on tax law, fill out unintelligible forms, assess penalties if required, and submit this information to the government in a timely fashion.

This is a remarkably clever ploy. It saves the government billions of dollars by not having to hire tax collectors—people to fill out these forms for us. All they need to hire are tax enforcers—also known as the IRS.

We have accepted this role for far too long. Apologists for the IRS, of course, would say that it is our duty to serve as our own tax collector. This is a specious argument. It is our duty to pay fair and reasonable taxes; it is *not* our duty to have to collect them from ourselves. It is a grossly unfair burden.

Actually, this setup is part of the shell game. We are expected to collect and submit our own taxes, but then the tax laws are made so complex that it is an impossibility for the average citizen to prepare the annual tax forms. If you ask twenty different tax experts a question on tax law, chances are excellent that you will get twenty different answers—and all of them will be wrong.

Nor is the IRS any help whatsoever. They will give you advice, of course, if you call them and are willing to wait fifteen minutes for a line to open up. But they take no responsibility for giving you wrong information. If you act on their advice and the decision is reversed by a tax examiner, it is no excuse to claim that you were given this information by the IRS! You still have to pay the penalties and fines.

(For this reason, always request advice from the IRS in writing. New laws require the IRS to honor any opinions given by IRS agents to tax-payers in writing.)

Even precedent, which is hallowed in our judicial system, carries no weight in dealing with the IRS. My wife and I were first audited in 1983; the audit examined our 1981 tax return. It lasted four hours and included extensive discussion of one deduction we had taken for charitable contributions. At the end of the audit, the examiner found that our return was in proper order, the deduction was correct, and that we did not owe anything. She praised me for the clarity with which I presented our records.

Four years later, in 1987, we were audited again—an audit that lasted five years and eventually covered six years of tax returns. The same issue came up fairly early in the audit. I explained the basis for the deduction and then added, "This issue was thoroughly reviewed in an audit in 1983, not just by the examiner but also by her supervisor. My decision to take the deduction was upheld by that audit."

The examiner looked at me and said, "That doesn't matter. Rulings in previous audits apply only to that audit. They set no precedent for future audits." Then he added an ominous note:

"We don't even have a copy of your previous audit on file."

Why not, I wondered.

"It would take too much storage space to keep everyone's old tax returns," came the answer.

Apparently the IRS has never heard of microfilm.

I tried to explain that this peculiar quirk of the IRS was at complete odds with 200 years of judicial tradition in this country, plus several hundred more in Great Britain, but it didn't matter. Once you start dealing with the IRS, you quickly learn: they are a law unto themselves. None of your normal rights and privileges as an American citizen will help you now.

In point of fact, the IRS had changed its ruling on my deduction in the four years since the first audit. This was a minor ruling that had never been published in any major newspaper or magazine or reported on television; it took my tax lawyer substantial research in order to find the ruling in question. But as obscure as it was, my wife and I were expected to know about it and prepare our tax returns accordingly. Our examiner was ready to assess us a huge penalty for having the audacity to take a deduction that the IRS had approved in our last audit!

This is why it is unfair to make us our own tax collectors. The average American citizen is neither an accountant nor a lawyer. The tax forms and instructions are so complicated that anyone who tries to fill them out himself is running an incredible risk of flunking an audit— or being slapped with a huge penalty for not knowing what to do. Ignorance of the law is not accepted as an excuse by the IRS, even though the tax manual used by the IRS consists of 260 volumes of small print! The only reasonable option is to take your tax returns to an H&R Block or similar tax firm—or to a tax lawyer. In other words, we are forced to pay someone else— and a good tax lawyer gets paid as much as $175 or more an hour—to make sure that we can perform our enforced duty as tax collector.

In this way, the king has his cake and eats it, too. We end up paying for the government's army of tax collectors, and never even know it.

In fact, we continue to believe that the pea is under one of the three shells. We have accepted our role as tax collector without thinking about it. Which, of course, is the underlying problem. If we start thinking about it, we won't put up with it any longer.

An argument could be made that it is better for us to be our own tax collectors rather than to have to deal with yet another level of IRS bureaucracy. This is probably true. But if we are going to continue to act as Uncle Sam's tax collection force, we ought to demand some simple changes:

1. We should demand simpler tax forms and rules, so that the average citizen with a high school diploma can comfortably and quickly fill

it out, without fear of being liable for horrendous penalties.

2. We should demand less grandstanding by the IRS—the yearly charade of publicly prosecuting some well-known figure just before tax time, so that we will all be sufficiently intimidated when we sit down to do our taxes.

3. We should demand tax laws that do not change every year, making it impossible for us to stay abreast of the current tax law. The constant changes in the law and the forms are a tremendous burden on all of us taxpayers.

4. We should demand tax forms and tax laws that can be easily understood—and are unambiguous.

5. We should demand that as tax collectors as well as taxpayers, we should enjoy the presumption of innocence until we are proven guilty. This basic right of American citizenship has never been adopted by the IRS in the way it treats the average taxpayer. I have had taxes, penalties, and fines levied against me, and backed up with the threat of the seizure of property, without any hearing or due process. In dealing with the IRS, there are times when sane people

begin to think that we actually lost World War II. It is not in the best interest of any American citizen to let this condition continue.

6. We should demand more restrictions on the powers of the IRS, especially in the assessment of penalties and the seizure of property.

7. We should demand accountability and penalties for malfeasance and illegal harassment by IRS agents.

Writing in the 17th Century, philosopher Adam Smith postulated that one of the four most important criteria of any income tax is that it should pose no burden other than the tax itself on the taxpayer. In other words, it should be easy to pay and easy to comply with.

This fundamental principle of taxation has been completely devastated by our modern system. It can be restored—but we will have to take the responsibility for demanding change, if change is to occur.

Why We Pay Taxes

As Adam Smith first postulated 225 years ago, there is one and only one reason for paying taxes: to raise revenues for the government. No other reason is valid. Nor should it be tolerated by the taxpayer.

This idea was commonly accepted in the 19th century, and even in the early years of the 20th century, when the income tax was first established. But political winds shift. A lot of politicians have found it convenient to forget the wisdom of Adam Smith.

If the only reason why we paid taxes was to raise money, our tax forms could be the essence of simplicity. Only four lines would be required:

1. A line on which you state your total income.

2. A line on which you deduct the exemptions you and your family are entitled to. Exemptions

represent the amount of money you can make before being liable to pay taxes. It keeps the poor from being taxed on the little they earn.

3. A line on which you state the percentage at which your income is to be taxed.

4. The amount of tax due, calculated by subtracting item 2 from item 1 and multiplying it by item 3.

What could be easier? Taxes could be calculated in less than five minutes. It would save the taxpayer a tremendous amount of time—and the government a tremendous amount of paper. Imagine—your whole tax return on one half of one side of one sheet of paper!

Unfortunately, the tax code has been hijacked and is being held hostage by certain politicians who just cannot refrain from using taxation for more than raising revenue. These politicians see taxation as a way of controlling the economy—and what is even more disturbing—shaping society.

This is why we have so many changes in the tax law, year after year, and so many forms to fill out. They are the ultimate result of politicians wanting to coerce us into doing what we may or may not want to do. Of course, they don't want to come right out and pass a law *forcing* us to do anything—that would be undemocratic. So they tamper with taxation, and give us incentives to do what we may not want to do. They believe we'll never figure it out.

It's the same old shell game, over and over again.

It's bad enough when the politicians use taxation to tinker with the economy. The assumption here is that too much inflation or too little growth results from bad decisions by the consuming public. Either we aren't buying enough or we're using too much credit—or both. So the government uses tax cuts to expand the economy, and takes the cuts back five years later to control inflation. It gives corporations investment credits one year—then rescinds them the next. And we applaud them, thinking they are controlling the economy.

Somewhere along the line, we are overlooking a simple, basic fact of life. Where is the intelligence in letting a group of people—known as Congress—tinker with the economy, when they cannot even balance their own budget? Congress has produced a national debt of more than one trillion dollars. It has shown no ability to eliminate this debt. If something is wrong with the economy, why does it try to solve it on the back of the taxpayer? Doesn't common sense suggest that it ought to clean up its own house first—by reducing the amount it spends?

Even worse is the bad habit of Congress to use taxation to shape society. It does this through the complicated mass of deductions and credits it has written into the tax code—the very things that make filling out your tax forms difficult and onerous.

My wife and I happen to own a home. Naturally, we take our full deduction of mortgage interest when it comes to filling out our tax forms. But for the life of me, I cannot understand why I am entitled to this deduction, whereas people who rent are not.

The "reason" why is, of course, simple. Congress, bowing to the pressure of the building industry, has decided it wants to encourage home ownership. So it gives a deduction that makes it extremely desirable to own a home—even if you don't want to.

This is social manipulation—and it is the one and only reason why your tax form is so complex. If Congress were forbidden from using taxation for social engineering, your tax return could be as simple as I described it at the beginning of this chapter.

Actually, there is reason to believe that this kind of social engineering is unconstitutional, although the principle has probably never been tested in the courts. In 1924, the U.S. Supreme Court, in Bailey vs. the Drexel Furniture Company, declared a tax act unconstitutional because it imposed a tax on violations of child labor laws. Under the law that was struck down, the profits of any company knowingly employing minors would be taxed ten percent for the years of the infraction. In writing its opinion, the court stated that preventing companies from employing minors was an issue of criminal law, not taxation; the law was a police regulation, not a legitimate form of raising revenue. In supporting this decision, the Court cited the tenth amendment to the Constitution, which states:

The powers not delegated to the United States by the Constitution, nor prohibited by it to the States, are reserved to the States respectively, or to the people.

In other words, the Supreme Court has ruled, based on this amendment (the last of the Bill of Rights), that all the Thirteenth Amendment authorizes Congress to do is establish a tax system for the collection of revenue. It does not authorize Congress to use that tax system for any purpose other than raising revenue.

Since deductions and tax credits are not a necessary part of raising revenue, they may well be unconstitutional. I qualify the statement in this way, due to the unusual way in which our courts work. The Supreme Court does not rule on laws as such; it rules on the application of laws to specific cases. As long as no specific cases come before the court challenging the social engineering aspects of the income tax, or the ways in which the IRS applies them, we the people have no way of knowing what is constitutional and what is not. All we can do is make educated guesses.

Whether the immensely complicated system of deductions, credits, and special provisions is constitutional, however, one fact still remains.

The Congress and IRS have made tax collection far more confusing and convoluted than it needs to be. All we need to do is eliminate all deductions and credits, and our lives will be instantly made much easier.

But if we actually did eliminate all these deductions and credits, wouldn't our taxes go up? Not if our representatives and senators wanted to stay in office.

Under the present system, the tax rate is set higher than it needs to be, to give Congress room to extend all of these deductions which make us feel so good. If we eliminated all of the deductions, the tax rates could be dropped as well. I am not an actuary, so I can only guess how much they might drop. The bottom rate of 15 percent might drop to 10 percent; the top rate of 31 percent might drop to 25 percent. Better mathematicians than I can figure it out in a flash. But on the average, everyone would end up paying the same amount of taxes as they do now—because the government needs the same amount of revenue. The only difference is that it would cut out the hypocrisy of our tax system—and make filing our tax returns a simple operation.

I would eliminate all deductions except one: the deduction for charitable contributions. Charities, after all, perform work and services that government would probably decide to do if there were no charities. So it is important to continue the deduction for charitable giving, as it represents our only true choice of whether this money is going to go to the government—or an activity we support. It is the one small way in which we can try to keep government from becoming any more massive—or pervasive—in our lives.

As for all the rest of the deductions and credits, I would trash them—as being so much baggage that ultimately does us no good. No more deductions for interest, health expenses, day care, age, or whatever. This suggestion is bound to send various special interest groups into hysteria, but there is one special interest group we've ignored for far too long:

The taxpayer.

Making the tax code as simple as possible is in the best interest of every American. Regardless of race, color, creed, or sex, we are all taxpayers.

Cha-Ching!

A popular television commercial for a fast food hamburger chain shows a family in their station wagon, ordering a meal at a competitor's drive-through window. As the clerk rings up each part of the order on the computer, he pumps his arm up and down, as though he were playing a slot machine, dances a little jig, and imitates the sound of an old-fashioned cash register: "Cha-ching!" When the full order has been made, he tallies it up with one final "cha-ching," and announces that the meals come to $62.75. Shocked, the driver of the car has to admit, "We're a little shy."

As taxpayers, we should identify with the driver in this commercial. Somehow, when the tally has been totalled, we are always a little shy—and we never know the reason why. We have been cha-chinged.

It's all part of the shell game—a deliberate effort by our government to pacify us into thinking that taxes aren't nearly as bad as they actually are.

After all, there are only three published income tax rates. Most people pay 15 percent after deductions. The more prosperous pay 28 percent. The rich pay 31 percent. But if you think that this is all that you, or anyone else pays, you are sorely mistaken. It's just the beginning.

First of all, there are Social Security and Medicare taxes—both the 7.65 percent that you pay and the 7.65 percent that your employer pays for you. Cha-ching.

Then there are federal unemployment taxes— again paid by the employer. This may be as much as 6 percent of your income. Cha-ching.

These are all income taxes—taxes assessed on the basis of your income. But there are other taxes to consider as well:

Taxes paid by corporations on the profit they make. Cha-ching.

Indirect federal taxes and levies. Cha-ching.

Inheritance taxes. Cha-ching.

Gift taxes. Cha-ching.

Taxes on gasoline. Cha-ching.

In all, in an average year, the total federal taxes collected from we the people amount to a whopping 43 percent of total personal income. That means that of every dollar you or I earn, 43 cents of it somehow ends up in the federal pocketbook.

That's a far cry from the 15 percent most of us believe we are paying in taxes. Cha-ching!

In fact, for the country as a whole, it amounts to more than one trillion dollars.

And that's not the whole story by any means.

We all live in states, most of which assess an income tax all of their own. This can eat up from 4 to 8 percent of your income. Cha-ching!

Most of us live in cities or communities that likewise have income taxes. In our neck of the woods, it's a flat two percent of total income (no deductions are allowed). Cha-ching!

If we own a house, there is also the property tax to pay. This is not based on income, of course, but the value of the house we can afford to own is largely determined by the amount of income we have, and the tax rate is based on the home's value. Among my friends and associates, property tax usually ends up amounting to 3 to 4 percent of total income. It will obviously be higher if property taxes are paid as well on investment holdings such as stocks and bonds. Cha-ching!

Every time we buy a car, new or used, taxes are paid to the state as well. Assuming that we buy a new car every three years, this amounts to another one percent of our income. Cha-ching!

And then there are all those other purchases which are subject to state and local sales tax. Cha-ching!

And the taxes we pay on food and lodging when we are travelling. Cha-ching!

As well as *state* unemployment and work-man's compensation taxes, in addition to what the federal government has charged. Cha-ching!

I am not a mathematician, so I cannot calculate precisely what the total tax bill represents in relation to our total income. But starting with the 43 percent we pay at the federal level, and adding the amounts enumerated above, the total rises quickly above 60 percent of total income for the average American taxpayer. In reality, it is closer to 65 percent than 60. Cha-ching!

This means that for every dollar we earn, more than 60 cents of it goes in taxes of one kind or another. That is four times the 15 percent most of us think we are paying. No wonder we feel a little shy!

This frightening statistic is dramatic proof of the shell game that is being played on us by our government. A one percent tax doesn't sound alarming. Even a five or ten percent tax doesn't sound too bad. Being good citizens, we are certainly willing to pay our share.

But 60 percent? More than half of our income? Isn't that outrageous?

I think so. Perhaps you do, too. But it's the truth. Three-fifths of everything we earn goes to taxes. Cha-ching!

To put this another way, everything we earn working Monday, Tuesday, and Wednesday goes to the government at one level or another. We are left with what we earn on Thursday and Friday to pay our mortgage, buy groceries, send the kids through college, and save for retirement.

Compare this with the tax burden in 1900. It was less than 5 percent. It was paid off in just a couple of hours on Monday. Actually, the state and local governments collected twice as much in taxes as the federal government did. Now the situation is just the opposite.

I do not profess to know what a reasonable tax burden is, but I do know an unreasonable one when I see it. Or pay it. And 60 percent—or more—is unreasonable.

I would like to think that it is also unAmerican, except that it is happening right here in the U.S. It's been happening for 50 years.

When this country was founded, it was conceived as the citadel of free enterprise. One hundred years ago, philosophers started using other terms, like capitalism.

In a pure capitalist society, there would be no taxes. All money that was earned would be available for investment as capital. Zero taxation, of course, is impractical, but for most of our history, the total tax burden on the American taxpayer has been less than 10 percent—usually less than five percent. So the ideal can be approached, and government still operate.

In a pure socialist society, there would be no personal income. Taxes would be 100 percent. Living allowances are distributed by the state to the individual, but all property belongs to the government. There is no capital. This system has been tried by such advanced communist nations as the former Soviet Union, and found to be unworkable. Nonetheless, there are socialistic societies that approach the extreme. In Sweden, for instance, 90 percent of all income goes to taxes.

Where does this place us—America in the 1990's—on the sliding scale between capitalism and socialism? Alas, we must conclude that with 60 percent taxation, we are a lot closer to socialism than we are to capitalism.

We still think of ourselves as a capitalist society, of course, and pretend to be engaged in free enterprise. But the truth is patently clear. We have become a socialist state. The tax bill proves it.

It was not communist agents who killed capitalism. It was not the robber barons who so many people feared. It was our own government, through the means of an out-of-control tax system.

Capitalism is dead, at least in this country. It has been killed by taxes.

Cha-ching.

Double Trouble

One of the slickest tricks in the shell game of American taxation is double taxation. This is something like having a contractor remodel your home, only to be charged the full amount of the work both at the beginning and the end of the job! It's a nice scam if you can pull it off.

Unfortunately, the U.S. government does pull it off, cheating us of billions every year. It works this scam in part through the corporate tax.

Corporations are groups of individual citizens who come together for the purpose of manufacturing and selling a product or providing a service. If a corporation makes a profit during the year, the entire profit is taxed. Some of this profit, perhaps all of it, is then distributed among the shareholders who own the corporation. They report it as income—and pay tax on it once again.

The monies that are distributed to shareholders in this country are all double-taxed in this way. This means that if you own any stock—even through a profit sharing program in the company you work for—you end up paying a double tax.

If you are a shareholder in a company that makes a profit of $100 per share, for instance, and pays you a dividend of $85 a share, the company will pay federal income taxes of $15 and you will pay federal income taxes of anywhere between $12.75 on the low end and $26.35 on the high end. That's as much as 41 percent, thanks to double taxation.

Most people, of course, think it's a great idea to tax corporations. After all, if the corporations weren't taxed, we'd all have to pay more—right?

Not right.

We end up paying corporate taxes anyway, in the form of higher prices for the goods and services we purchase from them. When corporations are required to pay a tax on profits, the only result is that some of the tax burden we bear is hidden, obscured. We start thinking that we only pay 15 percent in taxes, rather than 60 percent—or more.

The whole idea of corporations paying income taxes is alien to the principles of this country—most specifically, our treasured ideal of no taxation without representation. Corporations have no vote. If they have no vote, why should we expect them to pay taxes?

Double taxation is probably legal, but it is an idea that should repulse every thinking American citizen. What is fair about exposing the same income to the omnivorous bite of the IRS twice? Isn't this discrimination against the owners of stock?

There are a number of other forms of double taxation that are hidden by taxing corporations. The most obvious is social security. We pay 7.65 percent of our wages into social security—and so does our employer. You may think it's great that you only have to pay half of the social security tariff—but this is just another deception of the old shell game. Employers may pay for all kinds of special benefits, such as medical insurance, in addition to social security taxes. But if they weren't paying for these things on your behalf, they would have that much more available to pay you!

It doesn't matter which shell you look under—the pea won't be there. It's been palmed. Ultimately, we the taxpayers end up shouldering the bill, no matter how much Uncle Sam splits it up and hides the pieces.

The taxes your employer pays for workman's compensation and unemployment benefits fall into the same category. They are paid by corporations and employers—but they come out of your pay envelope. They are part of the total salary or wage expense your employer pays in exchange for your services.

One of the oldest double taxes, of course, is the inheritance tax, and its spinoff, the gift tax. It's like the corporate tax in many ways, except that it is tacked onto the other end of the process. Each year throughout your working career, you make a certain amount of money—and are taxed on it. You use the rest of it to buy groceries, pay the mortgage, put the kids through school, and so on. You may even save some of it—or invest in stocks. Of course, if you make any money on these investments, you pay tax on it.

When you die, the estate you leave behind represents your *net worth*. If your estate goes directly to your spouse, there are no taxes. If it goes to others, there will be a substantial exemption. But if the estate is large enough, there will be taxes to pay.

In order to avoid this tax, people started giving their wealth to family members and others in the form of gifts. The IRS responded by instituting the gift tax. Each year, we are allowed to give as much as $10,000 to any one person, tax free. Any amount over the $10,000 limit must be declared as income by the recipient.

Nor can you skirt this tax by forgiving debts owed by children or others. Any amount over $10,000 will be construed as income in the year the debt is forgiven.

Both the inheritance tax and the gift tax are, of course, double taxes. With the inheritance tax, the money is taxed first as income, and then later as net worth. But where did this net worth come from? Your income. With the gift tax, the money is taxed first as income and then later as a gift. But the money is just being transferred—not earned.

Inheritance taxes were well rooted in this country before the advent of the income tax, and

I am not naïve enough to believe that our government would ever willingly let go of one tax just because it had found a new and better one. But most tax experts agree that it is an inequity to tax the same funds twice.

I happen to be a big fan of the inheritance tax as the best way to keep money in circulation. I agree with Andrew Carnegie that while it is honorable to make huge sums of money, it is not honorable to die of old age with those huge sums in the bank. Wealth brings with it a responsibility to use the major share of it for the betterment of mankind, through charitable programs and gifts. If this responsibility is shirked, I see nothing wrong with government heavily taxing the remaining estate. But as long as inheritance taxes are coupled with an outrageously high income tax, double taxation will be inevitable.

And that means that the tax system is discriminatory and unfair.

The Paperwork Tax

Had I been alive in 1909, I surely would have opposed the introduction of the income tax. But I am a realist; I do not actually expect our society to jump back 80-some years and eliminate it entirely. The purpose of this book is to point out the unfair and even harmful aspects of the present tax system, in the hope of inspiring major reforms.

Obviously, the primary reform that is needed has little to do with the tax code. To lower our tax burden substantially, we must convince Congress to start spending less money. A lot less money. And that is a task almost as daunting as the one facing David as he stared at Goliath.

Many of the needed reforms have little to do with money, however. There are many ways the tax system could be made more humane and workable, even if we never were able to convince

Congress to rein in the runaway horse of spending.

To me, the most distasteful aspect of paying income tax is the immense amount of paperwork which must be filled out each year, as we perform our ritual duties as unwilling tax collectors.

My wife and I are by no means wealthy, yet our average 1040 tax return runs twenty pages—twenty pages to tell the IRS that we don't owe any more than it's already collected, and it doesn't owe us a refund. Taking twenty pages to say nothing strikes me as an awful waste of paper.

But it's not the paper that bothers me. It's the time and number of headaches it represents.

Each year, my wife and I dutifully save all kinds of receipts and records for one reason and one reason only: to substantiate our deductions to the IRS. At tax time, then, I collect all these records from various filing places, and transfer the appropriate figures and numbers onto the correct lines on my computer tax program.

(Like everyone else, I used to fill out my tax forms by hand. But filling out forms by computer is much, much easier. If you get a good program, it will remember all kinds of information from one year to the next. The computer also reduces the number of arithmetic mistakes.)

All of this takes time—lots of time. I estimate that we spend twenty hours each year just filling out the 1040.

State and local tax forms add several more hours. But in addition, we always seem to have two or three partnership returns to complete, and sometimes forms we've never heard about before. Add another 10 hours to the total.

The result is 30 hours of labor each year to do a job that should only require five minutes. I generally bill my time, when hired as a consultant, at $75 an hour. Using this figure, it costs me $2,250 each year in time to fill out the paperwork required by the tax system.

I consider this as much a tax as the money I have to pay. The sad thing is that it is just lost productivity. The government doesn't benefit from it, I don't benefit from it—no one does. It's a pure waste of time and energy. And an unnecessary waste at that. Under a fair and equitable tax system, it should only cost one hour of my time to file all my tax returns—state and local as well as federal. This was one of the key tenets of Adam Smith's philosophy.

As already mentioned, we have also been personally audited twice in the last decade. On the first occasion, I spent four hours gathering records and four hours answering the questions of the examiner. In this case, the paperwork tax amounted only to $600 or so. It probably cost the IRS $300 to conduct the audit.

The second audit started in June of 1987 and lasted until December of 1991. It began with the examination of just two years—1985 and 1986—but ended up encompassing 1987, 1988, 1989, and 1990 as well. The first visit lasted eight hours and accomplished almost nothing. Subsequent visits only made matters worse. I could see from the beginning that the examiner had no capacity to grasp the information I was presenting him—even though it was essentially the same as it had been four years earlier.

Conservatively, this second audit consumed a total of 80 hours of my time in gathering backup information requested by the IRS and another 80 hours meeting with IRS personnel. In other words, I had to suffer a paperwork tax of at least

$12,000—the value of the time required to convince the IRS no changes were necessary.

In addition, I also had to hire a tax lawyer to represent me during the last half of the proceedings. I made this decision after the fourth meeting, when the auditor accused me of criminal activities—a typical example of unfounded IRS harassment. Legal fees relating to completing the audit have cost us (in very real dollars) more than $10,000.

These are not typographical errors. I spent $12,000 of my time and $10,000 in legal fees in an exercise that concluded that we did not owe the IRS anything, and vice-versa.

I am naturally grateful that my returns were found to be accurate, but I happen to believe that forcing taxpayers to spend this much time and money to defend what is right is excessive. It's also ludicrous, absurd—and frightening.

I have no way of knowing what the IRS spent on this exercise, but it was surely in excess of $5,000. That's $5,000 of taxpayers' money to ascertain that my wife and I are honest people.

Unfortunately, our case iss not unusual. Thousands of Americans are subjected to this kind of expense every year, as the IRS tries to sniff out tax cheats. I know that some citizens do cheat on their taxes; some estimates claim that tax cheating robs the government of as much as 80 billion dollars each year. But these are estimates made by the IRS, who have a habit of grossly overstating the amount of taxes due. In our case, they claimed at one point that we owed a quarter of a million dollars in back taxes; in the end, they agreed we owed nothing. In another case I know of first hand, the IRS originally submitted a tax bill of $38,000; they eventually revised this figure down to $3,000. Case after case confirms this pattern. So it is ridiculous to believe that the American taxpayers are cheating Uncle Sam by $80 billion a year. Even eight billion dollars is probably much too high a figure. But that comes to less than one percent of the total taxes collected by the IRS.

I have never cheated on my taxes. But after the last audit, I feel I have been cheated—cheated by the IRS. It cost my wife and me $22,000 in order to prove that we were honest taxpayers who had submitted accurate tax returns. This is money we cannot recover—and no one at the IRS has volunteered to compensate us for our expenses.

If a burglar broke into our home and stole $22,000 worth of money and jewelry, we would be able to get the money back; our insurance company would compensate us for our loss. But when the thief is the IRS, the cost of jumping through their hoops is a loss without compensation. It is money that is gone.

This is one reason why I feel the Internal Revenue Service is the biggest tax cheat in America today—in fact, the biggest tax cheat in history.

The same problem, of course, occurs at the corporate level, only far worse. Companies have to hire departments of accountants and lawyers to handle the tax collection duties that have been forced onto them by the IRS.

Not only do they have to file the corporate equivalent of the 1040 (it's called the 1120) and pay tax on their profit, but they are responsible for filing many other forms as well:

• They have to make regular payments—weekly or monthly—of withholding and social security taxes due.

• They have to collect sales taxes and other taxes relating to their business.

• They have to file W-2's, I-9's, 1099's, and a whole bevy of other forms relating to their employees.

A small business, of less than 20 employees, may only have to hire one accountant to handle all this. But as the size of the company grows, so does the number of people needed to process this paperwork. Each of these people must be paid a salary and benefits. Yet they are not in any way involved in the manufacture, sale, or servicing of the product or service the company provides. This is a cost that must be borne solely to satisfy the IRS.

Once again, it is a totally unnecessary expense that cheats American business out of billions of dollars every year. It is the cost of supporting the IRS's shell game.

Probably the worst part of this dreadful system is withholding. Withholding was not part of the original income tax plan; it wasn't implemented until the 1940's. It was first suggested by Beardsley Ruml, who thought it would be much fairer to the average citizen, who frequently did not have enough money reserved, come April 15, to pay the tax bill he was confronted with.

Mr. Ruml undoubtedly had good intentions, but unfortunately they were of the kind used to pave the road to hell. By making corporate America the tax collector of withholding, not only has the IRS cleverly shifted the burden and expense of collecting taxes to the business world, it has become a major reason for the failure of businesses.

Not big businesses, as a rule of thumb—they have enough accountants to warn against getting into trouble. It is usually small businesses who fail from an acute case of IRS withholding. Here is how it happens:

John runs a store with monthly receipts of $25,000 and a payroll of $9,000. Every month he is expected to make payments of about $2,500 in income tax and social security withholdings. These are deposits that must be made through his bank. One month, he gets hit with extra expenses, and does not have enough cash on deposit on the day the taxes are due. So he cannot make his payment. If his cash crunch continues, several months may slip by. His debt to Uncle Sam grows bigger, and it becomes more and more difficult for him to recover.

The IRS, of course, doesn't view this money as a "debt"—they view it as delinquent taxes and treat John like a tax cheat. They give John an ultimatum he probably cannot meet, and then close his business down. They will also assess John, as owner, a penalty of 100 percent of the amount owed, which he must pay personally or face criminal charges.

All of this can happen without any opportunity for John to present his side of the case in court. He can eventually appeal the actions of the IRS, of course—but by the time he has a right to appeal, the IRS has already destroyed his business, his credit, and his reputation.

John, of course, never volunteered to withhold taxes. He was appointed tax collector 50 years ago when withholding was put into law. Seventy-five years ago, store owners and other small business people never had to worry about withholding. Now, it is a major cause of businesses closing their doors.

At any given point in time, some 350,000 businesses nationwide end up owing the IRS for back withholding. If half of them end up failing, that's 175,000 businesses a year put out of business by the IRS and made into criminals because they suffered from poor cash flow—because they had the audacity to risk their life savings to open a store or start a small business that would play its part in America's economy.

Being able to own and operate your own business used to be a central part of the American dream. Given the threat of the IRS, however, it is rapidly becoming part of the American nightmare.

As we will see in more detail, this is perhaps the greatest problem associated with taxes today. The IRS has the power to turn any American citizen into a criminal in a second—without trial, without due process of law, and without regard for rights we are guaranteed in the Constitution.

Any time 175,000 businesses a year fail for a single reason, Congress ought to investigate why. And since the cause can be traced back to a government agency they allegedly control, it is time for Congress to revise the withholding process, so that it works *with* businesses—instead of restricting and killing them.

A large part of the problem, both for individuals and businesses, is trying to keep up with the ever-shifting paperwork requirements of the IRS. I am associated with a small nonprofit corporation that was given its tax-exempt status by the IRS in 1980. At that time, nonprofit corporations were exempt not only from income taxes but also from social security withholding. The idea was that social security is a tax, and tax-exempt organizations could not be forced to pay a tax.

Two years later, Congress, hungry for additional revenues to spend, changed its mind. Social security might be a tax, it said, but tax-exempt organizations are going to have to pay it just like taxpaying businesses. Overnight, our payroll costs went up 15 percent. Our organization has never been able to fully recover from this change.

But, it turns out, other rules have changed in the last twelve years as well. Somewhere along the line, the IRS decided—but never bothered to notify us—that in a nonprofit organization, you must withhold taxes not just on wages paid to officers, but on any other payments to officers as well, just in case it slips their minds to report it on their tax returns.

As a result, our organization is facing $6,000

in penalties—even though we are exempt from paying taxes—because we failed to comply with a ruling that we were never notified of. The IRS agent who explained this to me freely confessed that almost no tax-exempt organization has known to comply with this change in rules—but this has not stopped the IRS from assessing and collecting the penalties.

We are not being assessed penalties because we failed to pay taxes. We don't owe taxes. We are not even being penalized because we withheld information. We are being penalized $6,000 simply because we did not use a particular form the IRS had mandated.

I don't expect anyone at the IRS to understand that nonprofit corporations are not run by accountants and lawyers trained in tax law. They are conducted, often at great sacrifice, by people who love what they are doing and care about their fellow human beings. Our only failure—not filing certain tax schedules we were unaware of—is certainly less damaging to America's welfare than a jaywalking ticket would be. Yet instead of $50 for jaywalking, we are being fined $6,000. For what?

For paperwork.

That's right, folks—we are now being taxed even for paperwork.

Sound like the Stamp Act 225 years ago? Perhaps it is time for another tea party—in Boston or wherever.

The Intimidation Tax

There's a subtle irony about modern taxes that should drive every American citizen right up the wall. Two hundred and twenty-five years ago, we fought a war of independence because we did not like the way King George III bullied us over taxes. Now, in the 1990's, we have created a tax monster that intimidates and bullies us far worse than King George ever did. And it is principally through this intimidation that the IRS cheats us—we the taxpayers—of billions of dollars every year.

Quite simply, the vast majority of American taxpayers are afraid to take all of the deductions the law entitles them to. They are afraid of being red flagged by the computer and called in for an audit—or they are just too timid to fight for deductions that are rightfully theirs.

The "red flag" syndrome is based on the fact

that the IRS cannot audit every single return. In fact, they audit only one percent of all returns each year. So they have built profiles into their computer. If your return falls into a high profile category—for example, if you take a deduction for an office in your home, or end up paying no income tax—your odds of being audited soar dramatically. If you have several red flags, you can almost count on being audited.

Keep in mind that a red flag does not mean that you have made a mistake or taken an illegal deduction. It simply means that you have fallen into a category that the IRS has found usually brings in additional revenue, if they audit the return. It's an area where people often make mistakes—or may be tempted to take more of a deduction than they are allowed.

The fear of being audited is so great for some people (and justifiably so, I am sorry to report) that they simply choose not to take deductions that will throw them into a high profile category. They would rather pay higher taxes than run the risk of an encounter with the IRS.

These people are letting the IRS cheat them out of billions of dollars each year.

But there is a second way in which IRS-phobia works—a way that is alien to every principle we hold to be American. Here's how this scam occurs:

Congress passes a new tax law. The IRS interprets it and establishes new regulations—which it disseminates to its agents, but probably not to taxpayers, unless it is a major issue.

You, the taxpayer, have heard something about what Congress did, and believe you are entitled to a deduction. You research the issue as fully as possible, and perhaps even call the IRS. The person answering the phone gives you an opinion—but there is no guarantee that it is based on official IRS policy. It may just be based on common sense—a very unreliable guide when it comes to taxes.

All evidence suggests that your deduction is valid, so you take it. In doing so, however, you are playing a dangerous game of Russian—er, American—roulette. If the IRS happens to agree with you, all is well. But if it disagrees with you, it will audit you and disallow the deduction. It will furthermore assess a penalty and charge you interest.

You can fight this decision, of course, but all the time you do, you are incurring more penalties and higher interest–unless you choose to pay the tax first and then sue the IRS to get it back. Sometimes this is feasible, if the tax due is low enough. But if the original tax bill is high– say, $40,000–you may not be able to scrape that together in time to satisfy the IRS. So you may have no choice but to fight them in court.

In the meantime, the cash register is cha-chinging away. Soon, your tax bill is $100,000; then $200,000. At some point, the IRS will get impatient. It may attach your salary and bank account, leaving you with too little to live on and wiping out your life savings. It may put liens on your house, ruining your credit. It may even seize your house and sell it.

In Tax Court, it is not up to the IRS to prove that you are guilty, as it would be if you were charged with theft, rape, or murder. Oh, no– you must prove that the IRS is wrong. You must suddenly become a tax code expert and prove that the IRS rules on this deduction are in error.

Surprisingly, this actually happens in a relatively high number of cases, because the IRS is very biased in the way they interpret the tax code. The IRS views each regulation in terms of how to get the most money out of us—not in terms of what Congress intended or what the words actually say. So taxpayers do win a lot of these cases.

The sad thing is that few of us are willing to pay the price of high legal fees and endure the brutality of the IRS to exercise our rights. So we give up without even fighting. We assume the IRS is right and we are wrong. We pay the bill.

This is what I call the intimidation tax. An investigation by the government's General Accounting Office in 1988 revealed that the IRS wrongly assessed penalties to 1.5 million taxpayers. Even worse, almost half of IRS mail to taxpayers contained errors regarding the amount of tax due. This is an outrageous situation and yet, because of the law, it falls to the taxpayer to prove that the IRS erred. The IRS can just stonewall it, and, in many cases, win.

Money magazine estimated that in 1989, of the $15.3 billion collected by the IRS in additional taxes and penalties, through audits, more than $7 billion of it was wrongfully collected.

How can this happen? We were bullied into

it, pure and simple. We think the IRS has the winning hand, so we capitulate, not knowing the true facts.

That's at least $7 billion stolen from America's taxpayers each and every year by the IRS. And the true figure is billions more.

This intimidation is not just a perverse accident or the paranoid accusation of a wronged taxpayer. It is an impression that is carefully created and sustained by the IRS itself. The IRS goes to great lengths to bust a number of famous people and corporations on tax charges just before April 15 each year. The message is clear: don't mess with us, or we'll bust you, too.

In fact, my research indicates that the charges are often knowingly trumped up. The IRS will send a corporation a tax notice of $112 million due in taxes two weeks before April 15, then four months later drop the claim. They never intended to collect the taxes—they just wanted to intimidate you and me. And by and large, they succeed.

Of course, it's not just you and me they are trying to bully. It's also our tax accountants and tax lawyers, starting with H & R Block and going all the way up the scale. These people know that if you are audited, they will have to explain why they took each and every deduction for you. In addition to the time involved, they may also face malpractice charges. So they won't take a lot of deductions you may well be entitled to—but they are unwilling to fight for. They are, in essence, working for the IRS, not for you—even though you get to foot the bill.

The greater the heat applied by the IRS, the fewer deductions these professionals will claim on your behalf. It's only human nature, of course—but it is another slick way that the IRS cheats us out of billions of dollars every year.

This excessive use of fear and intimidation may be appropriate for a dictatorship, but it has no place in the United States of America. It is time for Congress and the IRS to take steps to eliminate the intimidation tax entirely.

If not, I wouldn't be at all surprised if a citizens' tax group began campaigning for a new Constitutional amendment, making it only a misdemeanor to shoot IRS agents. After all, the Constitution does still protect our right to bear arms against menaces.

The Eliot Ness Monster

The stories of IRS malpractice are almost unending, but they need to be divided into two categories. In some cases, they are the result of individual arrogance and egomania on the part of just one or two excessively aggressive agents. Once the case goes to the appeals level, the problem is usually corrected. In other cases, however, the problem stems from agency policy. In other words, the IRS abuses the individual taxpayer with malice and deliberate forethought.

The first problem is far less disturbing than the second. In every business and government agency, there will always be those misguided individuals who assume far more power than they actually have—or abuse the trust that has been delegated to them. In our second audit, our major difficulty lay in dealing with an examiner of this kind—and a supervisor who had no reason backing him up. Of course, the arrogance of the supervisor may well explain the arrogance of the examiner.

In our first audit, our examiner could not have been more polite, helpful, and well-trained. She was thoroughly professional in every way. In fact, the afternoon was cordial, open, and frank. I was left with the impression that the IRS was trying hard to clean up its act—and treat taxpayers like the citizens they are.

This impression was quickly shattered in our second audit, the one that lasted for almost five years. It was clear from the very beginning that our examiner was acting on the assumption that we were crooks and that he had just been handed a plum. He was going to use this case to assess a huge tax bill and penalties, uncover a criminal conspiracy, and win a promotion.

Indeed, on any number of occasions he accused or intimated that I had indulged in illegal activities—a violation of IRS rules and regulations, since there was absolutely no evidence to suggest it. He also denied deductions that were perfectly legitimate and supported by tax records.

As the audit wore on, it should have become

clear that I was honest. The examiner would demand records, clearly expecting to find a smoking gun; I would produce them. Time after time, I validated every deduction I had claimed. But instead of perceiving a pattern of honesty, and bringing the audit to a close, he just got more and more frustrated. He wanted me to be a crook; he wanted his promotion.

He started asking for information that I had already supplied two or three times. He made promises that he later broke. Finally, he requested an on-site examination of our records. It was set for May 7, 1990.

A few weeks later, another IRS agent, who was working on an entirely different, corporate matter, scheduled an on-site appointment for May 6. She was unable to complete her work in one day, and indicated she would need to come back the next day. I did not want to have to try to deal with two IRS officers at the same time, so I called my attorney and asked him to arrange a postponement of our personal audit. This is a very routine procedure; he called the IRS and talked to the appointments secretary. There was no problem.

Except that our examiner showed up the next

day anyway, and proceeded to throw a temper tantrum. He then went back to his office and drew up a report that we owed something in the order of a quarter of a million dollars in taxes and penalties for three years.

We appealed the finding. After two hours of describing the treatment we had received, the IRS appeals officer agreed that there were serious problems in the way the audit had been conducted. He sent the case back down to the examination level, insisting that a new agent be assigned to the case.

Six months passed before the IRS could find an agent willing to take the case on. But the man to whom it was assigned was, like our first examiner, a decent human being. After only another year of presenting evidence and documentation—during which time the audit was expanded to encompass six years—we received our notice through the mail: the IRS had completed its audit and found no reason for charging us any additional taxes or penalties.

Of course, by this time we had spent $22,000 on legal fees and time defending ourselves against an incompetent, arrogant employee. But the system did have the ability to correct its own excesses—in our case.

There have been many other times, unfortunately, when the IRS has been unable to correct itself. Indeed, if I had not had the wisdom to hire an excellent lawyer, our case might well have become one of them.

Do you remember the movie, *The Untouchables?* It is the story of how Eliot Ness brought Al Capone to justice. The person who eventually nailed Capone and sent him to jail was not Ness, however, but a tax expert from the IRS who was assigned to help him. He used Capone's financial records to prove that he had grossly understated his income, and therefore was guilty of income tax evasion.

All of us undoubtedly applauded this clever trick when it was used on Al Capone, and for good reason. But exactly the same trick was used by our examiner to try to prove that we were crooks, not just ordinary honest taxpayers. Our examiner found that in one year, 1986, we had deposited over $500,000 in the bank, but only claimed income of $135,000. Obviously, he concluded, we had underreported our income;

obviously, we owed a whole lot of back taxes and fines.

He didn't bother to ask us about this, of course; he wrote it up as an official IRS report, then forced us to defend ourselves. Which was easy. We had bought a home in 1986 for $248,000. Instead of borrowing money from the bank, we borrowed money from family and friends—and paid cash for the home. But for a month or so before the closing, about $220,000 in borrowed money was sitting in our bank account. The rest of the money our agent misconstrued as income came from cash advances on credit cards and a line of credit.

Our examiner was so arrogant, in fact, that at one point he accused us of not reporting "casino earnings," as he called them, because a bank had labeled a cash advance as "CAS" on a report forwarded to the IRS.

My wife and I had never set foot in a casino, let alone ever gambled.

It is this Eliot Ness mentality that is the single greatest cause of taxpayer abuse by the IRS. And it may not be something that the IRS can purge itself of.

The IRS has its roots in the Bureau of Internal Revenue, which was started in 1862, when an income tax was first instituted, to help pay for the Civil War. That tax lasted only 10 years, but like so many government bureaucracies, the agency did not die when the purpose it was created to serve was discontinued. It was redeployed to collect tariffs, excise taxes, and so on.

In 1899, it was given the job of regulating drug trafficking in the United States. During Prohibition, it became the chief enforcer of the Volstead Act—which gave rise to the term *revenooer*, the IRS agent breaking up stills and raiding speakeasies. In 1934, it was selected to enforce the National Firearms Act.

These were reasonable decisions, because the income tax was still a fairly simple matter, even as late as the 1930's. Only five percent of the population was affected by it. It didn't overtax the IRS to collect back taxes and enforce all of these other laws.

But once the 1940's arrived, the whole complexion—and complexity—of the income tax changed. Suddenly, almost every householder had become a taxpayer, and businesses had been pressed into the service of withholding tax monies.

The IRS was no longer dealing with just gang-sters and crooks; they were primarily dealing with honest citizens. But they no longer knew how. In all too many cases, the mind set of busting Al Capone was the attitude with which they examined the records of teachers, car-penters, store owners, accountants, and other ordinary folk.

Even today, the mind set is still strong. In one IRS collections office, for example, there is a poster that says: "Seizure fever—catch it." This means that the IRS agents in that office are en-couraged to seize the property of taxpayers who have not yet even had a hearing in court. The Eliot Ness mentality lingers on.

In fact, it ought to be called the Eliot Ness monster, except that comparisons to the Loch Ness monster are inaccurate. As far as we know, the Loch Ness monster is mythical. The Eliot Ness monster is very real—and growing. And it cheats us out of billions of dollars every year.

Here are some cases illustrating why the Eliot Ness monster must be killed; it cannot just be restrained.

The most notorious of recent cases is that of Alex and Kay Council. I consider Alex Council to be a modern American martyr, a man who gave his life in order to expose the raving lunacy that can occur inside the IRS. This is not a case of an out-of-control agent; it is clearly the case of an out-of-control agency. Even the commissioner himself was out of control; after the IRS lost in court, he maintained that they had acted properly.

Alex Council was an accountant who had been a vice-president of a mortgage insurance company. He eventually went into business with his wife Kay while in their late forties. In 1979, Alex received a large bonus. He used some of it to make investments designed to postpone the tax consequences of the large windfall. One investment was in fine arts; before making the investment, Alex checked with his tax advisor and several lawyers, all of whom agreed it was a legitimate deduction.

Naturally, the IRS jumped on the deduction and ruled against it. The agent informed Alex by phone that she was not accepting it, and he would be billed for the taxes due. But Alex never received the bill. Nor did his tax advisor, to whom he had given power of attorney.

On all issues of personal taxes, there is a three-year statute of limitations. This means that the IRS must file a claim within three years or secure an extension from the taxpayer, or any claim is invalid. Alex and Kay received no such claim (it must be sent by certified mail, and the receipt must show it was delivered). So they figured that the agent had been overruled.

Six months after the statute of limitations had lapsed, they were shocked to receive notice from the IRS that they owed $183,021 in taxes, interest and penalties from their 1979 tax return. They contacted the IRS to try to find out what happened; no one responded.

For five long years, Alex and Kay battled with the IRS. The IRS finally claimed that notice had been sent within the three-year time period, but could not produce a copy of the certified mail slip. The Councils continued to claim they owed nothing; the IRS kept on running up the cash register. In the middle of 1987, for instance, they filed a tax lien against the Councils' property and assets for $284,718. Cha-ching!

This action drove Kay and Alex to the verge of bankruptcy, both personally and in their business. Their credit was ruined. They sought relief in court, but the court granted the IRS a delay to gather more information—after the case had been dragging on for four years!

When Alex saw that they were going to lose everything, he made what he called "a business decision." While Kay was out playing bingo, he went behind their house, put a pistol in his mouth, and shot himself.

This let Kay receive $250,000 in life insurance. Following instructions Alex had carefully written out before killing himself, she paid off enough debts to keep their business afloat. But even then the IRS did not back off.

Finally, six months after Alex committed suicide, a federal judge threw the IRS's case out of court and ordered the IRS to stop collection efforts and remove the lien on the Councils' house. He also awarded Kay more than $27,000 in legal fees.

Why? Because when the IRS finally produced the receipts of their mailings, it turned out they had sent them to the wrong address. A typo-

graphical error had caused the whole problem—
but it wasn't a typo that perpetuated it. It was the
Eliot Ness mind set of the IRS that killed Alex
Council—a man who knew he was right but saw
that he was trapped anyway.

In reviewing this case, it is important to realize
several key points:

• Had Alex and Kay Council been given the
same legal rights that we extend to rapists,
thieves, and murderers, Alex would have been
alive today. But unlike other law enforcement
officers, the IRS does not have to read taxpayers
their rights before taking action against them.
They can make innocent people into criminals,
just by *presuming* them guilty. They can ruin a
person's life over a typographical error, and then
claim, as the IRS commissioner did, that they
had done no wrong.

• The slowness by which the courts act en-
courages the IRS to perpetuate its barbaric, arrogant treatment of taxpayers. If the judge had felt
the need to give a delay to the IRS, why did he
not also issue an injunction preventing the IRS
from enforcing its lien during that time? It
would have given Alex and Kay some room in

which to reconstruct their business—short of suicide.

Incidentally, suing for such an injunction was not an option open to Alex and Kay, thanks to an obscure law called the Anti-Injunction Act of 1924, which gives the IRS much of its power to abuse taxpayers.

• Ultimately, whenever an intelligent person such as Alex Council feels the only way he can escape the trap of the IRS is through suicide— and events prove him to be correct—then the tax system has failed. It has failed to meet the points established 250 years ago by Adam Smith. The system has become an excessive burden on the taxpayer—not just Alex and Kay Council, but all of us. It is clearly time for reform.

A less spectacular, but equally disturbing case is that of Penny and Paul Stellmacher, which was reported in *Money* magazine. Without warning of any kind, Penny's employer received a demand from the IRS to garnish her paycheck to pay back taxes of $95,426. Before complying with the demand, however, Penny's employer advised her of the problem. She and her husband consulted a tax accountant who advised her employer to stop paying her until the matter was cleared up. Upon investigation, it turned out that the IRS had failed to register a change of name for Penny when she married Paul four years before. Since she had filed jointly with her husband, and not under her maiden name, the IRS incorrectly assumed that she had filed no return and owed taxes, penalties, and interest. Actually, she owed nothing.

Although the problem was straightened out quickly, it stands as another instance of IRS arrogance. No other agency of government would be allowed to breach the Stellmachers' constitutional rights in this way. But the IRS did it, is still allowed to do it, and continues to do it to unsuspecting, innocent taxpayers every day.

As Paul Stellmacher said, "They treated us like full-blown criminals." This is the way the IRS works; they shoot first, and ask questions later.

In some cases, the IRS has been known to seize the private records of physicians and other professionals, claiming they need them to assess taxes. But instead of asking for these records in writing, the IRS will sometimes just show up at the taxpayer's office with moving vans and haul away all of the filing cabinets on the premises. Not only does this violate the right to privacy of all of the patients or clients of the person involved, it often puts the taxpayer out of business until he or she can get the records back. How can a doctor treat a patient without his records of previous problems, medication, etc.? He can't. Nor can a lawyer or an accountant conduct business without his files.

We are supposed to be protected from this kind of seizure by the fourth amendment in the Bill of Rights, but so far the courts have failed to restrain the IRS. The IRS also seems unwilling to restrain itself.

One of the most notorious cases of taxpayer abuse involved the celebrated writer E.B. White, who received a notice just before April 15 of 1951 informing him that the IRS was going to seize his home in Maine because he owed $200 in taxes from 1948.

That's right—$200.

White wrote back a perfectly delightful letter telling the tax commissioner that since he was going to seize his home, he'd better know about the pregnant goose, who would need special care, where the dog was buried, and Mrs. Freethy's cookies, which White suggested he taste. He told the IRS everything he thought they would need to know about the property, writing in a warm, friendly tone. In other words, he demonstrated how a decent human being ought to act—something the IRS could not possibly know.

He then concluded his long and chatty letter: "I am sore about your note, which didn't seem friendly. I am a friendly taxpayer and do not think the government should take a threatening tone, at least until we have exchanged a couple of letters kicking the thing around. Then it might be all right to talk about selling the place, if I proved stubborn."

This incident occurred forty years ago, and the IRS still hasn't learned how to be friendly toward taxpayers. We aren't criminals, we aren't gangsters. We are the citizens of this country. If the IRS can't learn this lesson—and I'd give them another five years at the most to try—then I think the only solution is to disband the IRS and create a new agency to replace it, an agency that doesn't keep on trying to relive its glory days of trapping Al Capone.

The Sleeping
Watchdog

Part of the blame for why the IRS has been able to behave in these arrogant and brutal ways must be laid at the doorstep of the local and national media. When this country was founded, our forefathers guaranteed the freedom of the press, as a way of protecting against government abuse. For more than two centuries, in fact, the media has prided itself on being the watchdog of the government.

Sadly, it has failed its mission on the subject of taxation. In fact, it has become in many instances just an extension of the public relations arm of the IRS.

Each April, the IRS sets us up for its games of intimidation by making public a number of cases involving high profile individuals and corporations. It may be Redd Foxx one year and

Willie Nelson the next, but it seems as though there is always some big name being smeared through the papers.

These cases have generally been reported on TV and in the papers with the assumption that the IRS is right and the individuals are getting their just desserts. The cases become circus events instead of critical analyses of the facts.

The worst instance of pro-IRS bias in the media was the massacre of Leona Helmsley. *Time* magazine spent issue after issue gloating over her downfall, yet hardly ever bothered to mention the facts of the case. It is hard to understand how Leona could be guilty of tax evasion for a year in which she paid more taxes than most of us will ever pay during our whole lifetimes. She filed a return and paid a huge sum of taxes. She may have tried to claim a few deductions the IRS did not agree with, but is that grounds for tax evasion? How could she know how the IRS would rule—or the courts—until she tried to take them?

Leona Helmsley is obviously the kind of person many people love to hate. But she is still a citizen of the United States and deserves the same fair treatment every other taxpayer merits. If Leona can't get it, then why should any of the rest of us believe that we will be treated fairly, when it comes our turn to confront the taxman?

The answer is: we won't be. And the press is doing nothing to help make matters better.

Naturally, there are notable exceptions. The most impressive is *Money* magazine, which not only runs articles about IRS brutality on a regular basis but has even editorialized on the subject, insisting that it's time we all woke up. In fact, *Money* seems ready to spearhead a tax revolt. But on the whole, the press has played the sycophantic fool to the IRS. It has failed to report the brutal truth of IRS arrogance, badgering, and malfeasance, while serving as little more than a mouthpiece for IRS spokespeople.

A case in point is that of Alex and Kay Council. Until Alex actually committed suicide, no one would pay any attention to their story—including the press. The suicide changed things, temporarily—it was sensational enough to constitute news. But other than a couple of articles in magazines, there was little follow-up in the media. Hardly anyone in the press demanded that the IRS explain itself; it was all just a bad dream to be hidden under the bed.

Has the watchdog lost its bark? Not really. The press still knows how to complain about $900 screwdrivers. But when it comes to taxes and IRS abuse, it prefers not to look at the story. It rolls over and goes back to sleep.

Why is this? Part of it is probably just a large measure of very human cowardice. Journalists are taxpayers, after all. They undoubtedly fear that if they write unkind things about the IRS, the IRS will retaliate by doing unkind things to them. It has happened before, and is apt to happen again.

Indeed, as I talked to my friends about writing this book, they all thought I was crazy. "The IRS is gonna get you. You are really asking for it."

This may be true. But if it does come to pass, then it would be nothing but a confirmation of the truth of what I am writing. It also suggests that the IRS ought to reflect soberly on the nature of its reputation. After all, the unanimous opinion among my circle of friends is that the IRS is a mean-spirited, vengeful agency that is all too willing to stoop to the lowest level of indecency in order to retaliate against its critics. Whether or not it is true, this is certainly the perception of almost everyone I have talked to.

I can understand, therefore, why members of the press may be willing to pass on the watchdog role when it comes to taxes. They have families, careers, and homes, and do not want to lose them. So they look the other way.

But I suspect there is more to the story than fear. Most of the working members of the media support big government. The bigger government grows, the more important the media becomes, because it expands its watchdog role. Never mind the fact that the media isn't performing its role very well if government grows bigger; the media basically loves big government.

Big government requires big taxes, so the media is reluctant to be too critical of the IRS, lest they inspire a taxpayer revolt that shrinks the size of government—and thus the significance of the press.

This affection for big government is then magnified by a basic envy of the rich that clearly infiltrates every rank of the working press. Nothing gives the press more delight than taking part in the downfall of a) a big name politician, b) someone with a lot of money, or c) someone who combines both a and b.

What the media fails to understand is that these big name cases paraded before our eyes by the IRS and their dupes in the press are the way the IRS intimidates all the rest of us into playing the shell game. When it comes to taxes, we cannot afford to be envious of the rich. Only a very few of the very rich get nabbed by the IRS. After all, they can afford tax lawyers who ought to be smart enough not to get them into trouble with the IRS in the first place. But the IRS cleverly uses the few cases they do bring against the rich to lull the rest of us into a taxpayer coma.

Sooner or later, the audit lands on each of us or someone we know. At that point, we may begin to feel a distinct case of kinship with Willie Nelson, Redd Foxx, E.B. White, and even Leona Helmsley, no matter how unrich or unfamous we may be.

It may seem unfair to bash the media in this way, but the media is directly involved, whether it likes it or not. Our elected representatives have not yet gotten the message that meaningful tax reforms are still needed. Until they start reading it every day in the papers and hearing it every night on the evening news, they are not apt to get the message.

Some people might argue that we ought to go straight to Congress about these problems, not through the press. This sounds good, but what these people fail to understand is that Congress is guilty of putting an ever-increasing amount of pressure on the IRS to raise more revenues. Congress itself is a source of taxpayer abuse, and it is not apt to become a source of help until it feels the heat of a taxpayer's revolt, each day and every day through the press.

Twenty years ago, Howard Jarvis spearheaded a tax revolt in California by promoting Proposition 13, which severely cut government spending—and property taxes. In the early stages of Jarvis's campaign, the idea of such drastic cuts was ridiculed by the press, and Jarvis was portrayed as an eccentric from the land of the fruits and nuts. Only as it became clear that Jarvis was winning the support of the people did the press become courageous enough to start reporting the campaign fairly.

I do not expect the press to take the lead in true tax reform. But we can make it follow, if enough of us are willing to reteach it to fulfill its basic commitment: to serve as a watchdog of government. The whole government. Even the IRS.

What can individual taxpayers do? For one thing, when the press starts running and airing reports in March about tax cheating and related issues, put pressure on your local paper or broadcaster to print the real story about the IRS. Nag them until they realize there is a story out there that they have been missing.

The same thing can be done on a larger scale as well, not only with the news programs—and news magazine shows like 20-20 and 60 Minutes—but with talk shows like Oprah, Phil Donahue, and Geraldo. Why don't these shows tackle a real issue for once? Isn't the abuse of taxpayers by the IRS a far more serious issue than people who sleep with their former spouses after they are divorced?

Our Vanishing Rights

In the last decade or so, it has become an obsession with us as a nation to protect our ecology. We recycle our trash. We worry about the ozone. We use the back side of pieces of paper to save a tree. We stop construction on highways so that an endangered species can have a chance to survive.

It's mildly ironic that at the same time we have toiled so industriously to save vanishing wildlife, we have been blind to a much greater potential threat: our vanishing rights under the Constitution. The United States of America is the most perfectly balanced free society ever created. Yet we are letting our income tax system strip away our rights and plunder our freedoms.

This loss of freedom is not something which might happen in the future, if we fail to act. It has already happened. It may still be possible to reclaim it, but only if we act in concert—taxpayers and media—to demand that Congress restore these rights. We cannot afford to wait another ten or twenty years, to see what happens. Our rights under the law are being abused willfully and maliciously by the IRS every day. Unless this outrage is halted, freedom as we have known it will have no chance of surviving in this country, short of an outright revolution.

There are five articles in the Bill of Rights that have been trampled by the IRS with impunity. The first is Article IV, which guarantees our right to privacy and non-interference in our lives by the government:

The right of the people to be secure in their persons, houses, papers, and effects, against unreasonable searches and seizures, shall not be violated, and no Warrants shall issue, but upon probable cause, supported by Oath or affirmation, and particularly describing the place to be searched, and the persons or things to be seized.

I have been fortunate, thus far, not to have papers or property seized by the IRS. But I have had an IRS agent show up at my front door unannounced and enter my home to demand payment of "taxes" that were allegedly due from our business, even though the year in question had been audited and the auditor had found no such taxes owing. This agent had no warrant. A phone call could have worked just as easily as his invasion of my privacy.

But obviously Penny Stellmacher was not so lucky; the IRS tried to seize her property (her paycheck) without any advance knowledge of a problem on her part. They might claim that they thought they had probable cause, but the Constitution is quite specific. It does not allow for what the government "thinks" is probable cause; it demands the real thing.

Common sense alone should indicate that if a taxpayer has never caused any trouble before, and has always paid his or her taxes, probable cause does not exist. The taxpayer should always be given the benefit of the doubt, until it has been proven that he or she is a probable tax cheat. But this is not what happens now; the IRS assumes that the taxpayer is wrong, and they are right.

This is a pretty arrogant assumption, coming as it does from an agency that committed some kind of mistake on 50 percent of 36 million letters sent to taxpayers during a recent tax year. If anything is probable, it is that whatever the IRS has claimed, it is wrong.

During our several audits, I have been amazed at how readily the IRS, without our permission or knowledge, could summon and receive bank records, receipts, and even telephone records. Our privacy no longer exists; we are no longer "secure" in our houses, papers, and effects. The IRS treats the fourth article of the Bill of Rights as though it does not exist.

The same is true for parts of the fifth article, excerpted here:

No person shall be...compelled in any criminal case to be a witness against himself, nor be deprived of life, liberty, or property, without due process of law.

No tax examination begins as a criminal case, of course, but some of them end up that way, as Leona Helmsley discovered. Yet the tax laws force each of us to be a witness against ourselves—because it has made us each our own tax collector. This sets up an untenable conflict in regard to our constitutional rights. One way to resolve this dilemma would simply be to eliminate any criminal penalties for tax violations. Then the issue of testifying against ourselves would evaporate. It would also represent a giant step in helping the IRS recognize that taxpayers are citizens, not criminals.

The IRS also breaches the second half of article five by seizing property without due process of law. The term "due process of law" refers to the right to a trial once one has been charged with a crime or misdemeanor. But under IRS rules, taxpayers have no right to a trial until after the IRS has passed its judgment and the assessment has been paid. If you choose to exercise your normal right to a trial, the IRS will put a lien on your property—or just go ahead and seize it anyway. In many cases, the agents involved break agency rules as well as the law.

So why not sue them? It is, at last, becoming possible to sue the IRS—but so far no IRS agent has been held liable for his or her actions against taxpayers. This is an exemption we do not extend to police officers, tracking down criminals— why do we extend it to IRS agents who are harassing innocent citizens?

In fact, it is well known in IRS circles that collection officers seldom get promoted for being friendly and fair with taxpayers; they get promoted for seizing property and garnishing bank accounts, even when the action is not justified.

Another right that is regularly violated by the IRS is to be found in Article VIII of the Bill of Rights:

Excessive bail shall not be required, nor excessive fines imposed, nor cruel and unusual punishments inflicted.

This amendment notwithstanding, excessive fines and penalties have become a way of life for the IRS. In some cases, penalties can exceed 100 percent of the total assessment. If this is not excessive, it is hard to imagine what would be.

Penalties are assessed by IRS agents as freely as John D. Rockefeller used to pass out dimes to children. In most cases, the penalties assessed are far beyond the realm of reason.

Keep in mind that penalties are in addition to interest, which is also assessed.

At one point in our second audit, the original examiner issued a report stating that we owed

$51,000 in taxes for 1987—even though he had never audited our records for that year. On top of that, he added negligence penalties of $2,560 plus a penalty for substantial tax understatement of $12,798! This represents a penalty of 30 percent of what he claimed we owed!

I do not know precisely when a penalty or fine stops being reasonable and becomes excessive. But common sense alone should dictate that a 30 percent penalty—or even worse, a 100 percent penalty—is unreasonable, especially if the taxpayer has never been found owing taxes before.

In our state, the maximum interest that can be legally charged by banks is 24 percent; the maximum that can be charged by others is eight percent. Any interest higher than that is construed as usury. It seems to me that these might be adequate guidelines for tax penalties, too. Why not make 4 percent the standard penalty for most first-time tax offenses, with the penalty rising to 8 percent if the violation is flagrant, such as failing to file the 1040 at all? Second violations on the same issue could draw higher penalties, ranging from 8 to 24 percent, depending on the severity of the issue.

In our case, of course, we ended up paying no penalty at all, because the second examiner found no liabilities in our tax return for that year—or any of the six years examined. But was the first examiner held responsible for his incompetence and arrogance? To the best of my knowledge, no.

The last two articles in the Bill of Rights are perhaps the most powerful of all, especially in terms of tax rights:

IX. *The enumeration in the Constitution, of certain rights, shall not be construed to deny or disparage others retained by the people.*

X. *The powers not delegated to the United States by the Constitution, nor prohibited by it to the States, are reserved to the States respectively, or to the people.*

In other words, we the people retain any right that is not specifically yielded to the government through the Constitution or its amendments. Naturally, there can be wide differences of opinion as to what constitutes a right and what does not. Nevertheless, several observations can be made:

• The Constitution does not yield our right to rely on legal precedences. Even though this is not a right enumerated in the Bill of Rights, it is one of the hallmarks of our legal system. The IRS, however, ignores legal precedence as a matter of routine policy, unless the precedence originates from the Supreme Court. Simply by failing to take adverse decisions to the Supreme Court, the IRS can essentially remain a law unto itself. Here's how this scam works.

Taxpayer Jones takes an IRS ruling against him to a U.S. District Court and wins. The IRS has the option to appeal this decision to the Supreme Court, but if they lose at that level, they are bound to honor the deduction Jones took for every taxpayer in the nation. So they drop the case and honor it for Jones, and every other taxpayer in Jones's district. But they continue to deny the deduction elsewhere in the country—in the hope that a different judge will decide it differently.

If plain English means anything, this is a violation of the last two articles of the Bill of Rights.

On an even simpler level, the IRS does not even recognize a precedent established by its own audits. As reported earlier, our attempt to use our 1981 audit as a precedent for our second audit proved to be absolutely fruitless. This, again, flies squarely in the face of all legal process in this country.

• The IRS has become almost obsessed that all reports made to it must be on their forms. I have read the Constitution forwards and backwards, and have yet to discover where we the people yielded the right to communicate with the IRS in ways convenient to us, rather than to them.

Our nonprofit corporation, as mentioned earlier, is facing $6,000 worth of fines simply because we chose to communicate certain information in a way convenient to us, instead of using IRS forms. Making this choice did not cheat the IRS out of one dime of taxes. All income was duly reported by all parties concerned. But because the IRS is obsessed with making us a nation of bookkeepers, we are facing this penalty.

By my reading of the Bill of Rights, this is an unconstitutional intrusion into our affairs.

Our nonprofit corporation also received a warning from the IRS to keep more complete books, so that it will be easier for them to audit us in the future. This includes copying every check that comes in and keeping it, along with bank deposits, until they have had a chance to audit us. We were told that if our bookkeeping was still inadequate the next time they audit us, they could take away our tax-exempt status.

This threat also reeks of unconstitutionality. Our charitable purpose is not to spend a lot of money hiring accountants and lawyers to please the IRS—it's to promote specific educational goals. But the IRS doesn't care how much good we are doing in society—just whether we are making it easy for their agents to audit us! What a perversion!

• The income tax system has also produced a couple of side effects in society that have served to rob us of our freedoms and rights as citizens. If you have ever applied for a line of credit or loan at a bank, for instance, you will know that they generally request your tax returns for the last several years.

Our tax returns, of course, are supposed to be a private communication between ourselves and the IRS. This permits us to tell the IRS all kinds of private things we would never dream of announcing in public. But then banks turn around and demand to see the very returns which are supposed to be private.

I, for one, refuse to provide my tax returns— and the banks have to accept this refusal. I supply them with the information they need in other ways, such as verification of my employment and salary. But I see no reason why banks should have access to my tax returns. It is a basic violation of my privacy.

In one case, the bank said they would turn me down if I did not supply the tax return. I called their bluff and advised the banker to consult with his legal staff. One week later he called back and said the loan had been approved.

If we cherish our right to privacy, we have to take steps to protect it.

A less important example, except symbolically, involves our social security number. When the Social Security Act was first instituted, there was concern that we would all become a nation of numbers—a tremendous threat to our privacy and individuality. So the original social security cards clearly stated, "For social security and tax purposes—not for identification." This protected our basic right to privacy, at least to a degree.

•   My card still says this on it. But when my wife and I were married, she applied for a new social security card—one bearing her married name. It no longer had the protective line on it.

I do not recall voting to relinquish this right. So it must still be protected, under the tenth article of the Bill of Rights. But nobody else seems to think this way. The state puts it on my driver's license. The bank uses it to call up my checking account. I'm asked for it every time I want to cash a check at the grocery store. The insurance company uses it to process claims. Some people even have it printed on their checks!

How did this happen? Once again, IRS convenience became more important than taxpayer rights. The IRS decided we were hiding too much income in our savings accounts. So it introduced a requirement forcing banks to withhold a percentage of the income we make on savings accounts, unless we supply the bank with our social security number. And this invasion of our privacy opened the door of Pandora's box. Now everybody wants a social security number before they will do business with us.

The worst example of this came a few years ago when I went to a dentist for a checkup. He gave me a form to fill out. Right at the top, it asked for my social security number. I gave him back his form and walked out.

If we are ever going to stop the massive loss of freedom that is occurring in our country, we are going to have to take action.

My first recommendation is for every taxpayer to read the Constitution again—and the Bill of Rights. The last time most of us read it, if we ever have, was probably in school. Actually, I would recommend reading the Bill of Rights four or five times. Find out what your rights actually are.

My second recommendation is to stop letting people run over you and take your rights away. We have fallen into a stupor in which we believe that Constitutional rights are only for criminals. They are not. They are meant to protect the rights of ordinary citizens.

Above all, if you are audited or have to deal with the IRS in any way, bone up on your rights. If feasible or necessary, hire a lawyer and give him power of attorney to deal with the IRS. Agents tend to be far more polite in dealing with lawyers than individuals. They also know that they have to stick with the facts, and can't play the shell game of intimidation.

Our rights may well be vanishing—many of them have already been thrown away. But if common sense people decide that they have had enough of this nonsense, and band together, we can win them back. We can undo the damage that has been done.

We just have to be willing to work for it.

Mad as Hell

I first began writing this book with the intent of sharing with others my personal frustrations at dealing with the IRS, in the hope that it would awaken people to the realities of the tax system before they had to discover them first hand. But as I started to do research, to learn what others had experienced at the hands of the IRS, I began to get mad. As I pored through case after case of IRS malpractice and taxpayer abuse, I began to realize what a menace to our personal freedom the current system is.

I also became annoyed at the flaccid attitude of the press, which seems to be content to sit on its hands and do nothing, while one of the biggest scandals in the history of the United States continues to mount.

I thought of the Paddy Chayefsky movie *Network*, in which one of the primary characters, a

TV news anchor, gets fed up with the system that he has been a part of for so many years. On his newscast that night, he advises his viewers—if they agree with him—to go open a window, stick out their heads, and bellow, "I'm mad as hell and I'm not going to take this anymore."

I'm mad as hell, too. I hope you are as well. But it won't do us any good to scream it from our windows. We have to channel this indignation in constructive ways.

Some people, after all, get mad at the IRS or the tax system and just refuse to file income tax returns. This is not a good idea. In fact, it is counterproductive. The IRS will not accept your right to protest as a reason for not filing a tax return. You will just get slapped with a big penalty—and have to pay your taxes anyway.

There are more constructive steps that can be taken. One might be joining the National Taxpayer's Union, a group of 200,000 taxpayers who have united to present a common voice. Its address is: 325 Pennsylvania Avenue S.E., Washington, DC 20003. The phone number is (202) 543-1300. As more people join forces to battle tax abuse, the power of tax protest will increase.

If you prefer to act on your own, focus your efforts productively. Nag your local newspaper and TV stations to make tax abuse a major focus of their investigative work. Contact your representatives in Congress and encourage them to support genuine tax reforms.

If you don't know what to say in a letter to the editor or to your representative, here's a way to get started:

"I'm mad as hell, and I'm not going to take this anymore.

"The IRS is cheating us taxpayers out of billions of dollars every year. It has stolen from us freedoms and rights that our forefathers died to preserve.

"It's time to blow the whistle on taxpayer abuse, both by the IRS and Congress.

"What I want to know is just this: what are you going to do about it?"

If you want to be really dramatic, enclose a copy of this book with your letter. After the editor or senator receives a few dozen copies of the book, he or she is apt to wake up—and start thinking about what to do.

The simplest step to take is to start talking to friends, co-workers, and others about the need for genuine reform—of the tax code and the IRS.

Not everyone, of course, will agree. This is to be expected in a working democracy. People who have not suffered directly from IRS abuse may be tempted to believe that the charges are puffed up. Even if they accept them as true, they may be willing to endure taxpayer abuse as the price we must pay for enjoying government benefits. (In all likelihood, this means they are willing to endure it unless it happens to them.)

There are also people who like taxes, because they believe the income tax redistributes wealth from the rich to the poor. They are not rich, and so they support high taxes. The higher the taxes, the more the rich get penalized, right?

The trouble with this line of thinking is that it is 50 years out of date. Between 1913 and 1939, only the upper five percent of the population was taxed, and there was some shift in resources from the rich to the poor. But now the vast burden of taxation falls on the shoulders of the middle class. And the vast majority of cases of taxpayer abuse are directed at the middle class. Taxes are no longer an effective means for transferring income from the rich to the poor.

It is time to drop the excess baggage of worn out political ideology, and wake up to the danger at hand: if left unchecked, the IRS will destroy the rest of our freedoms—and it won't take them very much longer to do so.

It is therefore important that every citizen who values his or her freedoms—and wallets or purses—should become "mad as hell"—and do something about it. The issue is no longer taxes and who will pay for them. The issue is freedom—and how much longer we will have it.

Getting Relief

The idea of taxpayer relief is not a new one. Congress passed a law providing for a Taxpayer's Bill of Rights in 1988. It does provide a small measure of help, but not much true relief. For one thing, the version of the bill that was passed is just a shadow of the original proposal that was introduced. One by one, our representatives took out all of the real punch in the proposal. Second, we don't *need* a taxpayer's bill of rights. All we need is a directive that the IRS will respect the original Bill of Rights—and that we the taxpayers can sue to insure our protection under the Constitution at any stage that these rights are being violated. And third, even though Congress spelled out a few specific rights for taxpayers in this tepid piece of legislation, the IRS still routinely ignores them. In our audit, for instance, we had the "right" to request a new examiner at any time during the proceedings. But when we did so, his supervisor rejected our request—which left our attorney flabbergasted.

The one piece of good news is that the Taxpayer's Bill of Rights shows that some members of Congress are at least aware of the rising taxpayer resentment in this country. It is obvious, however, that they have no idea how important it is to provide genuine relief—and quickly.

There are two major issues involved: the level of taxes we pay and the way in which the IRS operates.

The first issue has nothing to do with the IRS; it falls entirely into the realm of Congress. Quite simply, we need to restrict Congress' ability to raise taxes, except in time of war. I would make the following proposals:

1. The government should announce and widely publicize each year what the total tax bite is for that year—federal, state, and local, including income, sales, excise, gift, corporate, and all other forms of taxes. This total should be compared with total personal income, as I did back in the chapter called "Cha-ching." This gives us an indicator of what the total tax bill actually

represents, as a percentage of gross income. At present, this figure is between 60 and 65 percent.

2. Congress should adopt a plan to bring this percentage of total tax to income somewhere under 50 percent, thereby halting the drift toward greater and greater socialism. I would set two targets: lowering the tax bite to 50 percent within 10 years and to 40 percent within 20 years. I would add that any elected official in a government unit (federal, state, or local) that failed to meet its goal would be forbidden from holding government office after that date.

If, after five years, Congress appears unwilling to act on these proposals on its own, I suggest a grass roots movement such as the one spearheaded by Howard Jarvis 20 years ago to translate these ideas into constitutional amendments.

The second issue deals with the policies and practices of the IRS. Here are a number of proposals that I think would bring well-deserved taxpayer relief:

1. All deductions should be eliminated, except the deduction for charitable contributions. To compensate for the loss of deductions, the basic tax rates would be lowered.

2. The implementation of proposal #1 would make it possible to simplify the tax return to six lines on the top half of one page. These six lines would cover:

a. Total income.

b. Charitable contributions.

c. Total exemptions allowed.

d. Tax rate, as defined by the instructions.

e. Tax owed, computed by subtracting b plus c from a and multiplying it by e.

f. Tax (or refund) due, computed by subtracting the amount of taxes already paid from d.

There could still be separate worksheets for the self-employed, rental income, and so on—but taxpayers should also be allowed to submit standard accounting balance sheets in lieu of IRS forms.

3. Taxpayers should be given a choice of how their taxes are to be collected.

Option #1—make quarterly payments on their own.

Option #2—allow the IRS to make automatic withdrawals from a checking or savings account, based on instructions given by the taxpaer with the tax return. The IRS would not be permitted to withdraw any amount greater than the sum specified; if it tried, the bank would have the duty to refuse payment until the taxpayer had been notified—and given his or her approval.

Option #3—have funds withheld by the employer, as is currently done, except that the employer would be reimbursed by the IRS for the costs of tax collection.

4. Penalties should be reduced. In specific, no penalty should be assessed to a taxpayer until after an audit or examination. No penalties should be applied to taxpayers who voluntarily amend their tax returns based on the receipt of new information, so long as the amendment is made within six months and such amendments do not occur more often than three times every five years. The maximum penalty for a first-time adjustment should be four percent of the amount in question. This amount could rise to eight percent for a second adjustment on the same issue, and twelve percent for additional adjustments on the same issue. The maximum penalty that should be allowed would be twenty-four percent. This should be reserved for truly flagrant offenses—such as repeated failure to file a 1040.

5. There should be "no stacking" of penalties. Under current regulations, the IRS can assess penalties every month a problem exists, up to a certain ceiling—without any obligation to notify the taxpayer that there is a problem. By stacking penalties in this way, the IRS can brutally punish unsuspecting taxpayers for errors they have no idea they have committed.

6. All criminal penalties should be removed from tax issues.

7. Taxpayers should be able to request advance rulings on specific deductions from the Tax Court. At present, we can request advance rulings from the IRS, but they are not binding and just give us the IRS's biased perspective. It is therefore important that we be able to request rulings from an independent court. If the IRS disagreed with the finding of such a court, it should be able to appeal it to a higher level—but in any event, it would be bound to the decision as it applied to taxpayers throughout the country. If a taxpayer disagreed with the findings of such a court, he could appeal it to a higher level under normal judicial rules.

8. The Anti-Injunction Act of 1924 should

GETTING RELIEF — 115

either be repealed or amended, to allow taxpayers to use the courts to enjoin the IRS from seizing property, issuing liens, or otherwise enforcing arbitrary actions.

9. Penalties collected by the IRS would not be considered taxes, but would go into a special fund, to be used to compensate taxpayers who have been mistreated by the IRS.

Many critics of the IRS would like to see specific agents liable for malpractice, just as doctors and lawyers are. This idea has merit, but is probably unworkable. A better plan is to establish a schedule of penalties levied on the IRS for infractions of the law or their own regulations.

For example, when an examiner assesses $38,000 in taxes on a couple, and it turns out that the couple only owes $3,000, I would assess the IRS a penalty of 8 percent of the difference. In this case, that would amount to a penalty of $2,800 due to the taxpayer, which would mean that the couple would only have to pay $200. This kind of penalty would instantly eliminate the capricious assessment of overblown tax bills by the IRS, a favorite trick of the agency. The full sum of $3,000 would still be paid into the tax fund, but $2,800 of it would come from the special fund.

The beauty of this plan is that it would also cut into the arrogance of the IRS—its tendency to reward agents who abuse taxpayers. A specific cost would be assessed for taxpayer abuse—and this would show up on the agent's record. Too many penalties would indicate that over aggression toward taxpayers can cost the IRS big bucks.

10. Taxpayers should be reimbursed for full legal fees in any case that they win in court. At present, legal fees are limited to $75 an hour. Many tax lawyers earn $175 an hour or more.

11. Once passed, tax laws should stand as passed without constant tampering, thereby allowing for intelligent tax planning. Tax laws should have a minimum life of 10 years before they can be revised, except in cases where the taxpayers petition Congress directly for redress.

12. All forms of double taxation should be eliminated.

13. If required by law to withhold taxes, businesses should be given the option of postponing the timely payment of these taxes a) by notifying the IRS in advance of its intent, and b)

paying a 15 percent interest rate for this consideration. At no time, however, would a business be permitted to fall behind more than six months on its payments; if it did, then penalties would be assessed and the account would have to be brought current within 90 days.

14.	Interest paid to taxpayers by the IRS should be at the same rate as that paid by taxpayers to the IRS. At present, the IRS charges a higher rate of interest than it pays.

15.	The IRS *must* assign a new examiner or agent if the taxpayer complains about mistreatment from the one originally assigned. This would apply even in the collection stage of tax cases.

16.	If taxpayers who are being audited cannot afford a lawyer to represent them, they should be able to petition the Tax Court to appoint a lawyer for them. The lawyer would be paid by monies from the IRS penalty fund.

17.	If it becomes evident that a taxpayer is being audited and harassed for political or malicious reasons, the taxpayer should have the right to sue the IRS for damages of three times the greatest amount he or she has been assessed.

User Friendly

To some people, it may seem an impossible task to try to convince Congress to implement the changes outlined in the last chapter—or ones which accomplish the same thing. Over the years, the IRS has accumulated an immense amount of power—yet so had the central government of the Soviet Union. But all that power couldn't hold the nation together when the will of the people was aroused.

This is the secret of democracy: all of the power that the IRS seems to have was given to it by us—the taxpayers—either directly or through Congress. What we have given away can be reclaimed, if our will is great enough and strong enough.

The longer we wait, however, the harder it becomes to reclaim everything we have lost.

We just have to decide: we the people of this great nation deserve better treatment than we receive at the hands of the IRS. Either they reform themselves, from within, or we will impose reforms, from without.

By the same token, those politicians who spearhead genuine tax reform will be remembered and rewarded. Those who stand in its way will be remembered and dismissed from office.

The model for tax reform should be Howard Jarvis, who led the successful campaign for tax reform in California. When he began, he was labeled a crackpot and an oddball, but his message made sense. He was opposed by both parties in California and most of the special interest groups, and yet he prevailed.

The proposals I am making—and others have made besides me—are not nearly as radical as what Jarvis tried to do in California. They don't have to be. I am not calling for the dismantling of the IRS—unless they prove so intractable that there is no other way. Nor am I calling for the elimination of the income tax. There might be merit behind both of these ideas, but they are too radical. We need reform, not war.

I believe that every American is willing to pay fair and reasonable taxes collected under a fair and reasonable system. I also believe that every American should be repulsed by what has become standard operating procedures at the IRS.

I am certainly willing to pay my fair share. For the record, the proposals made in this book would *increase* my yearly taxes by at least $10,000. But I favor these changes because an unfair tax system unfairly taxes us all. It endangers the vitality of freedom in our country—an asset I would be willing to spend any amount of money to preserve.

When you reduce the proposals made in the last chapter to their essence, you end up with what E.B. White tried to instill in the IRS forty years ago: a measure of decency. We know that IRS agents are American citizens just like us. We know they have a job to do. But it is the kind of job that can be done in one of two ways: in a friendly, non-threatening manner, as proposed by E.B. White—or belligerently and maliciously.

It is time for the IRS to drop its Eliot Ness mentality and rejoin the human race. It is time for the IRS to teach its agents what it means to act as decent, friendly people.

Or, to put it in more modern terms, it is time

for the IRS and its agents to become "user friendly."

In computer lingo, user friendly is a term for computers that can be easily mastered by the average user. The concept extends to the company who made the system—or the software—having a friendly, helpful support team to assist frazzled users when things aren't working right.

As this concept might be applied to the IRS, it basically embraces the proposals made in this book. Forms need to be simplified. The demand on our time needs to be sharply decreased. Harassment and brutality need to be eliminated. But most of all, IRS agents need to learn to be friendly in dealing with taxpayers.

This is not political advice. It is just common sense. We all know about the golden rule. Treat other people as you would like them to treat you.

The first great step toward reform in the IRS could be accomplished if the IRS commissioner would just instruct his employees to follow the golden rule in all dealings with taxpayers. Before taking any action, they should ask themselves: "How would I feel if this action were taken against me?" If it would make them uncomfortable, intimidated, or brutalized, they shouldn't take it.

This doesn't mean that the IRS should drop all efforts at collecting past due taxes. Taxpayers do make mistakes; some do cheat. These people sometimes need a bit of encouragement to pay what they owe. But even unpleasant news can be delivered in a friendly, supportive way—if the person makes the effort.

I am a realist. I recognize that some IRS agents would have a hard time shifting gears in this way—although I believe most of them would rejoice in being able to treat their fellow Americans decently. I would not leave the agents on their own. I would provide them with the courses and training they need in order to make the transition from fire-breathing, arrogant gunslingers to cooperative, friendly advisors to the American taxpayer.

Becoming user friendly would not mean that the IRS had gone soft. It would just mean that it had discovered a more effective way of dealing with the American public. It would still be their business to collect taxes—and in a timely manner. But any attitude that assumed we are guilty, or treated us like crooks, would be completely out of place—and unacceptable.

As the editors of *Money* said last year, the IRS is "horribly out of control." As citizens of this country, this gives us a choice. We can sit on our rear ends and do nothing, while the IRS continues to careen recklessly, cheating us out of billions of dollars every year, robbing us of our basic freedoms as Americans, and terrorizing the lives of taxpayers at random. Or, we can band together to push both Congress and the IRS to adopt these changes, both in attitude and the law.

There is something for all of us to do. For some of us, it may be most appropriate to talk about the need for tax reform among our friends— to tell them the real facts about taxpayer abuse.

Others among us may have the opportunity to tell the message of tax reform to the local newspaper editor or TV news producer. Of course, every one of us has the right to write to our representatives in Congress and tell them: "I'm mad as hell, and I'm not going to take this anymore."

Perhaps the most important venue for promoting these changes will come with the annual ritual of filling out our tax forms. I would never

encourage anyone to take an illegal deduction—
that is tax suicide. But I would encourage everyone not to be intimidated by the IRS. Take the
deductions you feel you are entitled to; just make
sure you have the documentation to prove them.

If you receive communications from the IRS
about your return, do not just assume that they
are right. Double check their calculations before
you pay any claim for taxes due. Remember: the
IRS makes mistakes in half the letters they send
out every year.

If you are called in for an audit, don't let the
IRS intimidate you. It is not a foregone conclusion
that you will have to pay additional taxes. If
necessary, hire a lawyer to protect your interests.
And don't just assume that the IRS is right.
Chances are 50-50 that there is an error in their
assessment—an error that will favor you, once
you correct it.

But even if you are not audited, tax reform
should be important to you. Stand up and be
counted, in the media and with your representatives to Congress. Let's make this an issue—in
this year's election and in every election until fair
tax reforms are implemented. Check the voting

record of your representatives on tax reform issues. If it is unsatisfactory, press them to explain why. Ask their challengers how they would vote on tax reform. Demand specific proposals.

Don't be blinded by the fact that the coming election is a Presidential one. It is Congress that passes tax laws and controls the IRS. It is in Congress that true tax reform will either flourish—or be ignored. So we must take care to elect representatives and senators who will push for true tax fairness—and user friendliness.

If Congress does not act, it may be necessary to go to the grass roots and initiate a campaign for one or more Constitutional amendments. If this is necessary, then it is important for each of us to do our share, when the time is right.

If you are ever going to get mad as hell about taxes, now is the time to do it. We have to stand up and say, "We aren't going to take this anymore! We aren't going to let the IRS continue to cheat us for one more day!"

Let's make sure Alex Council did not die in vain. It may be the best gift we can give our children—not just the gift of fair taxes, but even more importantly, the gift of our basic rights as citizens.

A Sample Letter

I'm mad as hell, and I'm not going to take it anymore!

The Internal Revenue Service is cheating us taxpayers out of billions of dollars every year. It has stolen from us freedoms and rights that our forefathers died to preserve.

More than $7 billion is illegally collected every year from taxpayers who do not owe it. Billions more are stolen from us through intimidation, double taxation, and excessive paperwork.

The IRS has become a brutal, insensitive agency that routinely mistreats taxpayers. Rapists, thieves, and murders have more rights under the law than honest taxpayers.

Taxes are too damn high.

It's time to blow the whistle on taxpayer abuse, both by the IRS and by Congress.

What I want to know is just this: what are you going to do about it?

(Permission is granted to photocopy this page)

Another book from Enthea Press:

The Tao of Meow

by Waldo Japussy

A brilliant parody of the classic Chinese text, *The Tao Te Ching,* as told from the purrspective of a wise cat. Witty, charming, and poign- ant—a wonderful gift.

$14.50 plus $1.50 for shipping.

Order Form

❑ Please send me ____ copies of *The Biggest Tax Cheat.*
❑ Please send me ____ copies of *Fart Proudly.*
❑ Please send me ____ copies of *The Tao of Meow.*

❑ I enclose a check or money order for the full amount due (please include shipping charges and applicable taxes.)
❑ Please charge the order to VISA, MasterCard, or American Express.

Acct. No. _____ Expires _____

Please ship these books to (please print):

Name _____

Address _____

City/State/Zip _____

Enthea Press, P.O. Box 249, Canal Winchester, OH 43110